NATIONAL GEOGRAPHIC

READING EXPEDITIONS®

EYEWITNESS

The Johnstown Flood

D1604605

By Rebecca L. Johnson
Illustrated by Ken Call

Picture Credits
4, 7, 20, 32, 37, 40, 42, 45, 51, 54, 62, (icon art) Rick Wheeler; 4 Courtesy of the Johnstown Area Heritage Association; 5 (top to bottom) © Corbis; (map) Mapping Specialists, Ltd.; 62 © Corbis; 63 (diagram) Paul Perreault; 64 © Corbis; 65 © Bettman/Corbis; 66 (top to bottom) © Corbis, © Bettman/Corbis; 68 © Digital Stock.

Produced through the worldwide resources of the National Geographic Society, John M. Fahey, Jr., President and Chief Executive Officer; Gilbert M. Grosvenor, Chairman of the Board; Nina D. Hoffman, Executive Vice President and President, Books and Education Publishing Group.

Prepared by National Geographic School Publishing
Ericka Markman, Senior Vice President and President, Children's Books and Education Publishing Group; Steve Mico, Senior Vice President, Publisher, Editorial Director; Francis Downey, Executive Editor; Richard Easby, Editorial Manager; Bea Jackson, Director of Design; Cindy Olson, Art Director; Margaret Sidlosky, Director of Illustrations; Matt Wascavage, Manager of Publishing Services; Lisa Pergolizzi, Sean Philpotts, Production Managers, Ted Tucker, Production Specialist.

Manufacturing and Quality Control
Christopher A. Liedel, Chief Financial Officer; Phillip L. Schlosser, Director; Clifton M. Brown III, Manager.

Editors
Barbara Seeber, Mary Anne Wengel

Book Development
Morrison BookWorks LLC

Book Design
Steven Curtis Design

Art Direction
Dan Banks, Project Design Company

Published by the National Geographic Society
1145 17th Street, N.W.
Washington, D.C. 20036-4688

ISBN: 0-7922-5863-0

2010 2009 2008 2007 2006
1 2 3 4 5 6 7 8 9 10 11 12 13 14 15

CONTENTS

Johnstown, PA

IN 1889, flooding was not a strange occurrence to the people of Johnstown, Pennsylvania. Every year the Little Conemaugh and Stonycreek Rivers overflowed with meltwater from the Appalachian Mountains, causing the streets of Johnstown to flood. The Johnstown community rushed to save important possessions by moving them to the upper floors of their homes. The people stayed safely above ground until the flooding subsided. No one expected the heavy rains of May 1889 to cause worse flooding than usual. Besides, if the water of Lake Conemaugh rose too high, surely the South Fork Dam could hold it back.

▲ **Behind the houses and trees, the South Fork Dam holds back the water of Lake Conemaugh.**

▲ The people of Johnstown experienced flooding every year.

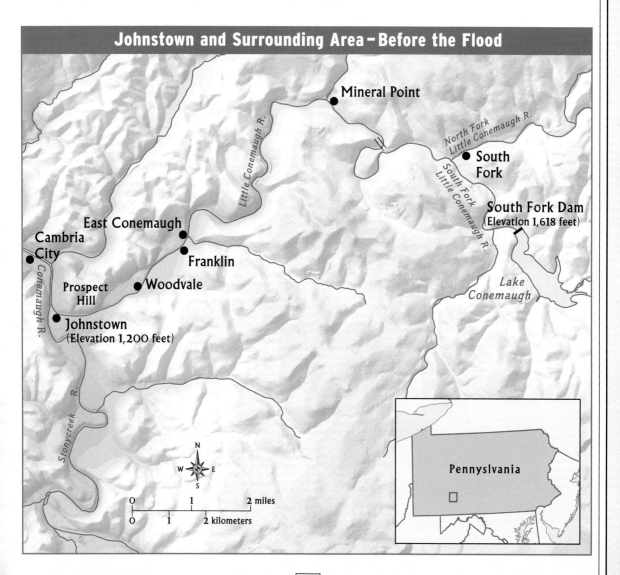

Johnstown and Surrounding Area – Before the Flood

Mineral Point

North Fork Little Conemaugh R.

South Fork

Little Conemaugh R.

South Fork Little Conemaugh R.

South Fork Dam
(Elevation 1,618 feet)

East Conemaugh

Cambria City

Franklin

Lake Conemaugh

Prospect Hill

Woodvale

Conemaugh R.

Johnstown
(Elevation 1,200 feet)

Stonycreek R.

N
W   E
S

0   1   2 miles
0   1   2 kilometers

Pennyslvania

CHAPTER 1

Johnstown

 THE LIGHT RAIN felt cold on Karl's face as he walked along Main Street. It was late May 1889, but still cold enough to make him shiver. He wanted to turn up the collar of his coat, but both his hands were full of packages. Karl glanced at his mother. She had her hands full, too, carrying Anna. He could see his baby sister's bright blue eyes peeking out from the soft woolen blanket.

The street was crowded. It was Saturday afternoon and many of the people of Johnstown were out doing their weekly shopping. So far Karl and his mother had been to the butcher, the baker, and the green-grocer. Their last stop was Heiser's dry goods store.

A young man in a bowler hat was coming toward them, splashing through the puddles. *"Guten Tag, Frau Edelmann. Und Karl,"* he called out. It was their neighbor, Mr. Rausch.

Gertrude Edelmann stopped and smiled. People pushed past them on either side. *"Guten Tag, Herr Rausch,"* she replied. *"Was machen Sie . . . ?"*

Before his mother could say another word, Karl interrupted. "Good day to you, Mr. Rausch," Karl said in English, a little too loudly. "You must have the day off. Are you out shopping, too?"

Karl saw the look of confusion pass over Mr. Rausch's face. The man smiled awkwardly. He obviously didn't understand what Karl had said. *"Ja, ja!"* he said after a moment, nodding. Then he smiled at them both again and headed off down the street.

"Karl," his mother hissed, grabbing his arm, "that was rude. You know that Mr. Rausch speaks no English yet. He just arrived here a few weeks ago. Speak to him in German."

"No, Mother," Karl replied. "We are Americans now. I think we should speak English."

Gertrude eyed her son sternly. They had had this argument before. Karl had picked up English amazingly fast after they'd emigrated from Germany to Pennsylvania last year. In Karl's school, all the classes were taught in English. Most of his friends spoke English, too. So it wasn't long before Karl was speaking the language very well. Gertrude and Karl's father, however, were still struggling with English. "I am glad that English comes so easily for you," she said softly in German. "But don't forget your native tongue. No one language is better than any other."

Karl stared down at the water that covered the street. He heard the anger in his mother's voice. But he was angry, too. He knew he had been rude. But every time his parents or their friends spoke German, he wanted to shout. This was a new country. And Karl so desperately wanted to fit in.

Karl heard his mother sigh. She let go of his arm. *"Kommst du!"* she commanded. She turned and began weaving her way through the crowd.

Karl followed. He was tall for twelve, and his legs were long. Gertrude was hurrying, but Karl had no trouble keeping up.

Heiser's dry goods store was two blocks north of Main, on Washington Street. As they turned onto Washington, Karl glanced up at Prospect Hill. It loomed over this part of town. Today the steep hill was just a gray shadow in the misty rain.

Johnstown was surrounded by dark green hills. The town was between two small rivers, the Little Conemaugh on the north, and the Stonycreek on the south. The rivers came together on the west end of town, near an area of land called "the Point." Together they formed the Conemaugh River. The Conemaugh wound its way north to the Allegheny River, which flowed through Pittsburgh.

Johnstown wasn't alone in the valley. It was surrounded by nearly a dozen little townships, or boroughs, as people called them. Some lay in the upper part of the valley, such as Woodvale, East Conemaugh, and Franklin. Others, like Prospect and Cambria City, were in the lower part of the valley. But there were no real dividing lines between all these places. They were all clustered together to form one thriving, growing community. During the 1880s, the population of Johnstown grew quickly. By the spring of 1889, nearly 30,000 people were living in and around Johnstown.

Karl loved Johnstown. There was so much to see and do. Several five-story office buildings stood on Main Street, along with dozens of shops. The town had a library and several schools. There were many churches: Catholic, Methodist, Presbyterian, and German Lutheran. Johnstown had a hospital, even an opera house. And at night, many of the streets were lit up by electric lights!

As Karl and his mother approached the dry goods store, Karl could see that it was very busy. People were streaming in and out of the big front door. Karl followed his mother inside. It was warm and smelled of tobacco and spices, licorice and gumdrops. Karl set his packages down and brushed the water from his coat. His mother was already at the counter.

"*Bitte, zwei* ... pound ... crackers," Gertrude began in broken English. "*Und ein* pound ... *Zucker.*"

"She wants two pounds of crackers and one pound of sugar," Karl explained to the big man behind the counter. Karl could feel his frustration building again. Every week his mother bought these things. Why couldn't she remember the English words?

The mist had changed to rain by the time Karl and his mother left the store. They hurried home, trying to avoid the worst of the mud in the streets. It had been like this last spring, too. Spring rains had soaked the city and the hills around it. The water had trickled down steep hillsides, filling creeks and streams. The Stonycreek and Little Conemaugh Rivers had swelled to overflowing, even sending water into the some of the streets. Karl's father had shaken his head when he saw this, saying that's what happened when people built a town on a **floodplain.** The neighbors all told them they would get used to it. Johnstown had flooded at least once each spring for as long as most of them could remember.

The Edelmanns lived at the eastern end of Washington Street, near the bottom of Green Hill. Karl loved to climb to the top of Green Hill and look at the view.

Karl ran up the front steps of their small house. It was like most of the other houses in the neighborhood. It was made of wood, small and neat, with a white picket fence around the tiny front yard. Like the Edelmanns, most of the people who lived in this part of town were recent immigrants. Many had come from Germany. Others came from Wales and Ireland.

He unlocked the front door and opened it for his mother. Both of them were soaked and spattered with mud. Karl took the packages of food into the little kitchen and set them on the table. His mother took Anna upstairs, to change the baby's diaper and to put on some dry clothes.

"Karl," his mother said, as she came down the stairs, "your father will be off work soon. I want you to go down and meet him. He will be hungry. You can take

---

floodplain – level land that may be submerged by floodwaters

him some *kuchen*." Gertrude cut a large slice of apple cake and wrapped it in a napkin. "Keep it inside your coat so it doesn't get wet," she continued. "Dinner will be ready when you two get home."

Karl grabbed his coat again and headed back into the rain. His father was a steel worker at the Cambria Iron mill. The mill employed a lot of Johnstown's men, including their new neighbor, Mr. Rausch. The steel mill was at the other end of Johnstown, downstream along the Conemaugh from the Point. Karl had a long walk ahead of him. But he didn't mind. The big houses were along the way.

Johnstown was a booming town. People who had good businesses quickly became rich. Many of Johnstown's wealthiest men had built big, expensive houses. Karl's favorite was the Morrell house on Main Street. Built by Daniel Johnson Morrell, a former manager of the Cambria Iron works, the enormous house was brick with a white roof. The house and its garden took up an entire city block. Despite the rain, Karl stopped to stare at the house through the black iron fence that surrounded it. He wondered what it would be like to live in such a house, with its grand veranda and huge glass windows that were taller than he was.

One day, Karl thought, *I'm going to be rich and live in a house like this. I'm going to be somebody.*

Reluctantly, Karl moved on. He didn't want to be late. After a few more blocks, he could hear the sound of rushing water. The Little Conemaugh River was running very high. The spring rains had been heavy. All the streams and rivers in the area were swollen with the rain that never seemed to stop falling. Karl would be happy when summer arrived, and rivers went back to their normal size.

Karl crossed a bridge that took him over to the bottom of Prospect Hill. He followed the river past the Point, where it joined Stonycreek River, and on down to the great stone bridge further downstream. Swirling, foaming brown water surged through the bridge's big arches. Karl stared at the water. It was moving so fast that it was a little scary. But it was rather exciting, too.

Beyond the stone bridge was the Cambria Iron Company. The sharp, burnt smell of the foundry hung thickly in the air. Tall smokestacks belched smoke and steam. They towered over the squat brick buildings of the foundry. Cambria made some of the best steel in the country. A lot of it became rails for the train tracks that were being laid all over the United States. Up in Woodvale, there was a factory that used Cambria steel to make barbed wire.

Karl hurried up to the high fence that surrounded the steel mill. A whistle blew. Moments later, men came

streaming out of an open doorway. Other men were on their way in. As one shift ended, another began. More than 7,000 men worked in the mill. It ran night and day.

Even through the rain and smoke, Karl spotted his father right away. Victor Edelmann was a giant of a man, tall and broad-shouldered. He walked with an easy grace. Victor was surprised and pleased when he saw his son waiting outside the fence. He strode over and threw a massive arm around Karl's shoulders.

"I've brought you something, Papa," Karl said. He pulled the *kuchen* from beneath his coat.

"*Danke, danke,*" said Victor, gratefully. He unwrapped the cake and took a huge bite. Two more bites and the cake was gone.

The rain had stopped. Father and son headed for home. As they walked, Victor told Karl about an accident that had happened in the mill that day. A man had been badly hurt. He spoke in German. Whenever Karl said something, he made sure to say it in English.

As they passed the stone bridge, Victor stopped to stare at the river. "*So hoch, so schnell,*" he muttered under his breath. The river was noticeably higher and moving faster than it had been when Victor walked past it early that morning.

"The bridge is strong enough to stand up to the water, isn't it, Papa?" Karl asked, wondering why his father seemed so concerned.

"*Ja,* Karl. This bridge is well-made," Victor replied. "But so much water, moving so fast. Not much can stand up to such a force. I once saw a flood-swollen river destroy a bridge made of iron. The water swept it away like a pile of matchsticks. People underestimate the power of moving water. They did back home. Here, too, I think."

"Back home." The words stung like a slap. Karl turned to look at his father. "Papa," he said, "America is our home."

Victor didn't say anything for a long time. He stared at the water, watching it foam and swirl. Finally he spoke. "Yes, Karl. America is our home now." Victor paused. "But there are things I miss about Germany. I miss building bridges."

Karl remembered his father working at his desk. He remembered the detailed drawings on big sheets of paper. Victor Edelmann had been an engineer back in Germany. He'd studied and trained for a long time, learning how to build bridges and dams and roads. When he received his university degree in engineering, Victor had landed a good job with a large bridge-building company in Frankfurt.

Frankfurt seemed very far away to Karl. He had liked many things about life there. But his parents had not agreed with the way the government was running the country. They were often outspoken. There had been threats made against the Edelmanns because of things that Victor had said. That's when Victor and Gertrude had decided to come to America. They had heard that in America, a person was free to speak his or her mind without getting into trouble with the government.

"I don't understand why you don't build bridges here, Father," Karl replied. "It would be a much better job than working at the mill. You'd make more money. We could live in a big house. People would respect us."

Surprised, Victor looked hard at his son. "Money doesn't make a person worthy of respect, Karl. Neither does a big house. Surely you know that."

Karl said nothing.

"Surely you also know," his father continued, "there are no jobs for engineers right now at the steel mill. If one comes up, I will try for it."

Karl remained silent. He knew his father worked hard. But who would hire a man as an engineer who only spoke a few words of English?

Victor was watching his son's face carefully. He put his hand on Karl's shoulder. "Karl," Victor said fiercely, "you seem ashamed of me!"

Karl looked at his father. "Um . . . no . . . well," he stammered. Then the words came very fast. "Perhaps if you spoke better English, Papa, you could get an engineering job here in Johnstown!"

Victor took a step backward. "Karl, you are ashamed of me!" he exclaimed bitterly. "*Ach,* Karl, Karl." Victor just looked at Karl and shook his head.

Karl could see the hurt in his father's eyes. He opened his mouth to speak. But Victor turned away and started walking. Karl followed in silence. Neither of them spoke another word on the way home.

Their silence lasted all through dinner. As soon as he finished eating, Karl escaped to his room on the second floor. He lay awake in his bed, unable to sleep. Karl knew he'd hurt his father. He knew he should apologize. But a part of him just couldn't.

I'll apologize tomorrow, Karl thought, burying his head in his pillow. Outside the rain began to fall again.

CHAPTER 2

The South Fork Dam

PALE SUNSHINE was streaming through the bedroom window. It had stopped raining, at least for a while. But Karl had overslept. He dressed and hurried downstairs. His mother was feeding Anna, but his father wasn't there. Then he remembered. His father worked. today. Many of the steel workers worked two Sundays out of every month.

"Mother," Karl began, "is Father still angry with me?"

Gertrude poked a spoonful of oatmeal into the baby's mouth. "He thinks you are ashamed of him, Karl," she said, looking at him sadly. "Your father is a good man. Why are you so critical of him lately? Of both of us?"

Karl didn't know what to say. His mother watched him for a few seconds before turning back to the baby. "I have a list of chores for you to do today. When you finish them, you can go and do whatever you want for the rest of the day."

Karl could hardly believe this. An afternoon to himself? "Thank you, Mother!" he said.

"Thank your father when he comes home. He thought maybe you needed some time to yourself, to think about what is important," his mother replied.

Karl worked hard to finish his chores by mid-morning. He was so excited to have a day to explore. He grabbed an apple and kissed his mother on the cheek. Then he bounded through the front door. "Be back for supper!" his mother called after him. Karl was down the steps before the door banged shut.

Karl practically ran down Washington Street. The cobblestones were wet and slippery from the previous night's rain. The air smelled of damp earth. Karl was tired of rain. He imagined that the rivers around Johnstown would be even fuller today. Karl stopped and looked up at the sky. He smiled to himself when he spotted a big patch of blue sky. Maybe the rains were ending!

By the time Karl reached the railroad depot across from Heiser's store, the sun was shining. Karl loved to watch the trains. One had just pulled into the station. Karl ran along the side of the train, past the passenger cars, then the boxcars and caboose.

"Karl, over here!" someone called hoarsely. Karl looked around. Crouching behind some bushes on the other side of the track were Peter Kraus and Patrick O'Hara. Peter was Karl's best friend. Karl didn't know Patrick well, but he'd played stickball with him before.

Karl ran over to the other boys. "C'mon, hide!" ordered Patrick. He reached up and pulled Karl behind the bushes.

"What are you doing?" Karl asked in a hushed voice.

"We're going to sneak onto the train and get a free ride up to South Fork," said Patrick with a grin. "Have you ever seen the dam up there?"

Sneak onto the train? See the dam? Karl hesitated. He wasn't sure these were things his parents would want him to do. But what an adventure!

"What's the matter? Are you scared?" Patrick asked, with a smirk on his face.

"Of course not," Karl retorted. "Count me in!"

Just then the train's whistle sounded. "Get ready," said Patrick, scanning the tracks. There was no sign of the brakeman or the stationmaster. "Now!" Patrick bolted for the closest freight car. Peter and Karl were close on his heels. The car's big sliding door was slightly ajar. The three boys shoved it open and hopped inside. They sat, catching their breath as the whistle blew again, and the train began to move.

The train headed northeast out of Johnstown. The tracks ran alongside the Little Conemaugh. The train chugged through Woodvale, then Franklin and East Conemaugh. From the doorway of the freight car, the boys watched the landscape roll past. Steep, wooded hills rose up sharply on either side. There were bare patches, though, where the trees had all been cut. The bare ground was cut with deep grooves where the rain had washed the soil away. Everything was damp or dripping.

Karl sat where the sun could shine on his face. Maybe the rains had finally stopped. He didn't think the land could possibly hold any more water.

South Fork lay a dozen or so miles from Johnstown. About 2,000 people lived there, in small clusters of simple houses perched on the hillside. As the train approached the station, Karl spotted a stream that joined the Little Conemaugh from the south. "What's that?" he asked Patrick. He'd learned that Patrick had made this trip several times before.

"That's South Fork Creek," Patrick replied. "We'll be following it up to the dam."

The boys leaped from the boxcar as the train pulled in. Patrick led them to a dirt road that ran alongside the creek. The road was muddy and rutted from the heavy rains. After they'd been walking for a few minutes, a horse-drawn wooden cart came rumbling past. The farmer driving the cart was happy to give them a ride.

As they rounded the second big bend in the road, Patrick nudged Karl and pointed. Directly in front of them was the South Fork Dam. Karl never imagined it would be so big. The dam rose more than 70 feet above the valley floor. It was a huge mound of rocks and rubble, nearly 900 feet across.

Up on the left side of the dam, a small **spillway** had been cut through the solid rock of the hillside. A wide sheet of water was pouring over the spillway. It made a beautiful waterfall that tumbled down the rocky face of the dam all the way to the creek.

The cart rumbled slowly across a small bridge. Then the road climbed steeply up the face of the dam, right to the spillway. Now the road split. One fork crossed the spillway and continued around the east side of the lake.

---

spillway – a passage for surplus water to run over or around a dam

build a system of canals across these mountains. People thought it would be a way to move goods quickly across the mountains. Quicker than it would be by wagon, anyway. So the state hired an engineer, a man named William E. Morris, to design a dam to hold back South Fork Creek and make a lake here. It was going to be part of the canal system."

Karl looked out over the lake, trying to imagine cargo ships crossing it.

Patrick continued. "It took years to build the dam. Morris was a good engineer, and he wanted the dam to be strong. But just before the dam was completed in 1852, the Pennsylvania railroad finished laying a rail route over the mountains. That put the canal out of business just like that!" Patrick snapped his fingers for emphasis.

"So the dam and the lake were never really used," he went on. "About ten years after that, the mountains got a lot of rain, like this spring. Quite a bit of water backed up behind the dam. And then the dam broke."

"Was there a flood in the valley?" Karl asked.

"Naw," Patrick replied. "The lake was only half full and the outlet pipes slowly let water out from the base of the dam, so there wasn't flooding."

"I didn't see any pipes on the way up," said Peter.

"That's because they were removed a few years back," Patrick explained.

Patrick leaned closer to the two other boys. "So, after that the dam was abandoned. Big cracks formed in it. It didn't hold much water, only enough to make a shallow pond. Then, about ten years ago, a fellow by the name of Benjamin Ruff bought the whole thing. Rumor was that Ruff was going to rebuild the dam. But when he found out how much it would cost, he decided to repair it."

"Yeah, I heard about that from my dad," said Peter. "People from all over came to watch the repairs. They said it was a joke. There were big cracks in the dam, and Ruff just filled them with anything he could find—rocks, mud, and tree branches!"

"He even used horse manure!" cried Patrick, laughing. "After the repairs were made, the dam broke just about every time there were heavy rains. Ruff kept fixing it. Finally it seemed to hold, and enough water backed up to make the lake. They called it Lake Conemaugh."

Patrick chuckled. "Then they stocked it with fish and built the clubhouse. They built the bridge over the spillway. They put screens in the water under the bridge to keep the fish from escaping over the spillway. After that, the rich people started coming to vacation here during the summer."

A shadow fell across the lake. Karl looked up. The sun had disappeared behind a dark cloud. In fact, it looked like it was going to rain again.

"Do you think the dam could break again?" Karl asked Patrick.

"Every spring, when it rains really hard, people talk about the dam breaking," Patrick answered. "But it never has. It's become a big joke."

The boys started back as the first raindrops began to fall. At the edge of the dam, they waited in the trees for a few minutes to make sure the coast was clear. Then they sprinted back across the dam toward the spillway.

Karl was the last to cross. The lake looked different now. In the sunlight, it had been bright and shining. Now the water was the color of cold steel. Karl noticed something else about the water. It was only about three feet below the top of the dam. If he'd dared take the time, Karl could have reached down and touched the surface of Lake Conemaugh.

CHAPTER 3

Rising Water

 KARL DIDN'T TELL his parents about his adventure up at the dam. In fact, in the days that followed, he and his father said very little to each other. Several times Karl tried to apologize for what he'd said by the stone bridge. But he just couldn't seem to find the right words. And the stern, hurt look on his father's face made him turn away.

Maybe on Thursday, Karl thought to himself. Thursday was May 30, Memorial Day, 1889. School would be out. The mill would be closed, too. Victor would have a rare day off. Karl hoped there would be a chance to talk to his father alone.

School kept Karl busy that week. Every night he had homework. Then he had chores to do around the house. Before he knew it, Thursday had arrived. Karl was excited to celebrate the holiday. He especially wanted to see the Memorial Day parade!

At noon, people began gathering along Main Street to watch the parade. Clutching a small American flag, Karl led the way through the crowd. He found a good spot at a corner. His mother and father stood behind him, with Anna. Everyone was shouting and waving flags. The fire department marched past, then a drum corps and veterans from the Civil War. A big cheer went up as each group passed by.

It had been cloudy and windy all morning, but dry. As the parade ended, the rain began to fall again. It rained on and off for the rest of the day and into the evening. After dinner, Karl hoped to talk to his father. But when he finished dessert, Victor quietly excused himself. He put on his big coat and sat out on the porch, smoking his pipe. Karl just couldn't find the courage to follow him.

Curled up in his bed, Karl thought about what he should do. But he didn't know. He fell asleep as the rain fell harder, drumming on the roof in an unbroken rhythm.

Then a loud bump woke Karl from a deep sleep. It was still dark outside. From below, he heard another bump, followed by voices. What was going on?

Karl dressed and hurried downstairs. He found his mother and father moving the rug in the dining room.

"What's happening?" asked Karl.

"It's been raining all night, Karl," answered his father. "The cellar is nearly full. There's even water in the street. We need to move whatever we can upstairs, in case the water keeps rising."

Karl ran to look out the front window. He could hardly believe his eyes. Yellow-brown water, maybe six inches deep, was running down the street. It was lapping the lowest step up to the porch.

Victor came up behind his son and glanced outside. "Karl, give me a hand with this rug. Please carry it upstairs."

After moving the chairs and small tables, it was time for Victor to go to work. "Stay here and help your mother,

Karl," he said. "I doubt there will be school today. Not with all this water."

Victor pulled on his coat and hat and stepped out onto the porch. The sky was very dark, even though the sun was now up. The rain was coming down in sheets. He hesitated on the bottom step, watching the yellow brown water swirl past.

Just then a shout came from down the street. It was Mr. Rausch, driving a small wagon pulled by a frisky young horse. Mr. Rausch was on his way to the mill. "Victor!" Mr. Rausch called in German. "Wait there! I'll pick you up!"

Mr. Rausch drove the wagon right up to the front steps. Karl and his mother watched from the doorway as Victor leaped aboard. Karl heard his father ask Mr. Rausch where he'd gotten the horse and wagon, but he never heard the response. Mr. Rausch tapped the horse with the whip and the wagon sped off. The wheels left small wakes in the dark water.

Back inside, Karl helped his mother put her best china in boxes and carry them upstairs. Then he ran back to the window. It was still raining. The water was still rising. Several children were out playing in the flooded street, sailing toy boats.

Karl looked farther down the street. A man was coming, on horseback! It was his father! "Mother, come see!" Karl called. The horse came splashing up to the house, tossing its head. Victor jumped down. The water was halfway up to his knees. He tied the horse to the porch rail and leaped up onto the porch.

Victor was soaked to the skin. "The mill is closed," he said. "Men are needed to help their families. Mr. Rausch is helping some friends of his who live close to the river move to higher ground. He didn't need the horse. And the water is too high for the wagon."

Victor took off his hat and wiped the rain from his face. "It's getting worse," he added. "Downtown is completely flooded. The water is several feet deep in some places. Both rivers are rising about a foot an hour."

More than a foot an hour? Karl remembered how close the water of Lake Conemaugh had been to the top of the dam.

Karl's father was telling his mother they should get food and water and move up to the second floor. For a moment he stood silently, thinking of what to do. His father was already angry at him. He'd be angrier when he learned Karl had gone up to the dam. But Karl had to tell him what he'd seen.

"Papa, I think we should worry about the dam," Karl said.

His father stopped in midsentence. He turned to face Karl. "Why, Karl? What do you know?"

Karl took a deep breath. "I was up at the dam on Sunday. Patrick O'Hara and Peter and I hitched a train ride to South Fork. We went up to the dam. The water was very high. It couldn't have been more than three feet below the top of the dam."

Karl waited for his father to get angry. But when Victor spoke, his voice was strangely quiet and calm. "Karl, get your coat and hat. You and I are going to ride up to the South Fork Dam."

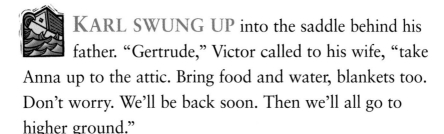 KARL SWUNG UP into the saddle behind his father. "Gertrude," Victor called to his wife, "take Anna up to the attic. Bring food and water, blankets too. Don't worry. We'll be back soon. Then we'll all go to higher ground."

The horse splashed down Washington Street, toward the depot. They crossed the bridge over the Little Conemaugh. The water was just inches from going over it. Victor gave the horse a kick. Karl tightened his grip on his father and they galloped up the valley beside the railroad tracks.

The rain was coming down in heavy, silvery sheets. Water was pouring down off the hillsides, cloudy and brown with dirt. It cascaded into the swollen river, which was a roiling mass of water that had spread far out beyond its banks.

The ride seemed to go on and on. But they reached South Fork in just over an hour. In ten more minutes they were at the dam. At its base, Victor pulled the horse up short. Water was shooting over the spillway, a great arc that soared into the air before crashing down onto the rocks. High overhead, they could see men moving back and forth along the edge of the dam. Victor urged the horse on. Moments later they were on top of the dam, looking at Lake Conemaugh.

Karl could hardly believe his eyes. The lake had looked big on Sunday. Now it was enormous. It had spread far up into the woods and fields that surrounded the lake. And it was no more than a foot from the top of the dam.

A crowd of men from South Fork were standing in the trees, next to the spillway. Along the road that crossed over the dam, about a dozen men were working with picks and shovels, trying to make the top of the dam a little higher. At the far end of the dam, men were trying to cut a new spillway through the hillside.

Victor swung down from the horse. He walked over to the men who were watching from the trees. He spoke to the men in German, asking questions about the dam. No one seemed to understand.

"Karl," he said sharply. "Ask them in English how fast the lake has been rising."

Karl translated the answer back into German for his father. An inch every ten minutes.

Victor turned and took Karl by the shoulders. He looked straight into Karl's eyes. "Karl," he said, his voice tight. "This dam won't hold much longer. Once the water goes over the top, it will fail. It's only a matter of time."

Karl's mind began to spin. The dam fail? All that water? His father shook him slightly. "Karl, you must not be afraid. I am going to stay here and see if I can help. We need to try to relieve the pressure of the water on the dam." He paused. "But you, my son, you must ride back to Johnstown as fast as you can. Get your mother and your sister and take them to higher ground. Take them to the top of Green Hill. And tell anyone that will listen that the South Fork Dam is going to break."

KARL HAD ONLY RIDDEN a horse a few times in his life. But he knew that everything depended on his getting back to Johnstown. As the horse thundered down the mud-slick road, Karl hung on for dear life. He reached South Fork in ten minutes. Not wanting to stop, Karl shouted at the top of his lungs as he raced through the main street, "The dam is going to break!" He saw several people smile and laugh.

The road back to Johnstown was even worse. The Little Conemaugh was rising steadily. In places, the water lapped at the railroad tracks. The ground was too muddy for the horse to gallop now. It was almost noon by the time Karl reached Johnstown. Nearly all the streets had water running through them now. The streets downtown were the worst. Karl guessed the water was ten feet deep in places.

People were hanging out of top story windows, watching him ride past. He called out that the dam was going to break. Most of the people laughed. They said they'd heard that joke before.

As Karl rode up to the house, he saw that the front porch was completely underwater. He jumped down from the horse. Muddy water swirled around his waist. He tied the reins securely to the porch rail and splashed into the flooded house.

In the dining room, water lapped at the bottom of the walls. "Mother! It's Karl!" he cried, taking the stairs two at a time.

He met his mother coming down from the attic. The look of relief on her face quickly turned to fear.

"Where is your father, Karl?"

"He's fine, Mother. He thinks the dam is going to break. He stayed to help." Karl grabbed his mother's hand. "But we need to get to higher ground. Right now!"

Minutes later, Karl was leading the horse down the street toward Green Hill. His mother sat stiffly in the saddle, with Anna locked in her arms. They moved slowly along, trying to avoid places where the water looked too deep. Once the horse almost reared as a big log swept past in the current.

The water got shallower as they neared Green Hill. Then they started up the hillside. It was a relief to be out of the water. But the steep hillside was slick with mud. Karl's mother got off the horse. It was too hard for him to carry her. She led the way up with Anna in her arms. Karl came behind, leading the horse.

Gertrude stopped to catch her breath. The water was streaming down her face. "How much higher, Karl?" she asked.

Karl looked down at Johnstown below them. "As high as we can get, Mother. As high as we can get."

 **AT LAKE CONEMAUGH,** Victor backed slowly away from the center of the dam. He watched the water slide across the top. Then it rolled over the edge, a huge, glassy sheet arching outward and down.

For several hours, Victor and the other men on the dam had tried everything to slow the rising water and relieve the growing pressure, but nothing had worked. Several men had been sent down to South Fork on horseback with warnings about the dam to be sent by telegraph to Johnstown, but the telegraph lines were down somewhere between South Fork and Johnstown. No one knew for sure if the message had gotten through.

The water pouring over the top of the dam was cutting deep into the outside face of the dam. The power of the water was incredible. It pushed away huge boulders. After just a few minutes it had carved out a great hole. Nothing could stop it. It was only a matter of time before the water gouged out so much of the face of

the dam that it would buckle under the pressure of the water behind it.

Victor heard shouts from the other side of the dam. Men were pointing to the dam's face. Victor scrambled up the hillside a few dozen feet to get a better view. There were cracks in the dam now. Water was surging through in several places.

Victor sat back on his heels in the rain. He took out his pocket watch. It was ten minutes past three. Karl should have gotten Gertrude and Anna safely to Green Hill. Victor tucked the watch back into his pocket. Then he stared in horror as the South Fork Dam simply gave way. Suddenly free to flow, millions of gallons of water thundered down into the valley below, heading for South Fork—and Johnstown.

CHAPTER 4

The Valley of Death

 THE RAIN was still coming down, but not as hard as before. Karl and his mother huddled together under the shelter of a large oak tree two-thirds the way up Green Hill. Anna lay tightly wrapped in a blanket between them. Gertrude had just fed her, and despite all that was happening, Anna had fallen asleep. Cold and mud-spattered, Karl and his mother were too tired to go further. The sun was low in the sky. It wouldn't be long before it was dark.

Karl leaned against the tree trunk with his head resting on his arms. He wondered what was happening up at the dam. Was his father all right? The strain of the ride back to Johnstown and the climb up the hill were beginning to show. Karl closed his eyes. He was suddenly very tired.

Karl's thoughts drifted back to his ride on the train up to South Fork four days earlier. It had been dark in the

freight car. The train had swayed gently back and forth. The wheels on the track had made a rumbling sound.

"Karl, Karl, wake up!"

Karl woke with a start. His mother was shaking him. The dream of the train vanished, but the rumbling noise was still there.

The sound seemed to be coming from up the valley. Karl strained to see through the failing light. The sound was growing louder and louder, turning into a roar like thunder. Then he saw an enormous wall of water that stretched from hill to hill. It had to be nearly forty feet high, and it was moving fast.

Karl felt rooted to the ground. He was so frightened he couldn't move. The wall of water was bearing down on East Conemaugh and Woodvale. As it churned forward, trees on the hillsides snapped off like matchsticks. The water reached the first houses. They were crushed like china cups. Several locomotives were swept up and tossed around like toys.

The wall of water hit the Gautier steel factory where the barbed wire was made. Karl saw an explosion of steam and black smoke. Then the factory was gone.

Beside him, Karl's mother was screaming. But the sound of her voice was drowned out by the terrifying roar coming from the mountain of water. Karl would have screamed, too. But he could hardly breathe.

The water kept coming, getting bigger and more frightening every second. Stores, streetcars, wagons, telegraph poles—everything was disappearing in front of it. The wall was almost through Woodvale now, heading straight toward the heart of Johnstown. Karl saw people moving down in the city, running for their lives.

The wall of water struck the eastern end of Washington Street with unbelievable force. Their house, Heiser's dry good store, and a hundred other buildings vanished. He saw a barn rolling along the front edge of the water like a barrel.

The water kept coming. Some of the tall brick buildings on Main Street collapsed like houses of cards. Smaller buildings were torn off their foundations. Karl watched in amazement as whole houses went swirling along, only to be smashed to bits when they crashed into other buildings.

Karl could see people in the water. Some were clinging to pieces of wood, trying desperately to keep their heads above water. Others climbed rooftops that had become temporary rafts. Some rooftops had overturned, and the people riding them simply disappeared beneath the water's brown, churning surface.

The water reached the center of town. The big houses that Karl admired so much caved in or were torn in half. The library disappeared. So did the Opera House. Karl saw the German Lutheran Church crumble at the same time the telegraph office was swept away.

The water kept moving on a straight path through Johnstown. It passed the Point and crossed Stonycreek River. Then it slammed into the hill that rose straight up behind the river. The sound was deafening. Unable to move ahead, the enormous mass of water and debris moved backwards like a wave receding after hitting the shore. The water seemed to split in two. One part rolled up Stonycreek, destroying everything on either side of the river. The other part surged back into Johnstown. A few buildings had survived the first wave. Now most of those were destroyed as the water returned.

People who had managed to climb onto floating rooftops were caught in the **backwash,** too. The returning water sent many of them spinning.

As the water ran out of power to move up the valley, gravity took hold. Now choked with an enormous collection of **debris,** it surged down the valley again. It was heading for the stone bridge.

When the water struck the bridge, Karl thought for sure the bridge would give way. But his father had been right. The stone bridge was strong. When the water

---

backwash – the forced backward flow or movement of water
debris – the remains of something broken or destroyed

struck, the bridge held. Torrents of water surged through the stone arches. But the debris began piling up. Boxcars, storefronts, trees, telegraph poles, pieces of thousands of houses, and miles of barbed wire from the Gautier factory were driven up against the bridge. Hundreds of people, both dead and alive, were trapped there, too. As the water kept coming, the debris piled up until it was almost higher than the bridge itself.

With the arches clogged, the water on the upstream side of the bridge had nowhere to go. It turned back toward town, creating a frightening whirlpool that spun slowly in a huge circle.

The deafening roar of the water was dying away. Karl heard his mother sobbing. Anna was crying. He heard crunching, grinding sounds as more and more debris piled up against the bridge. He also heard people screaming.

THE SUN HAD SLIPPED behind the hills. Darkness was falling. Through the gloom and the drizzle, Karl gazed out over a scene of utter desolation. The trapped water now formed a dark lake over much of Johnstown that was choked with wreckage. He could see a few chimneys sticking up above the water. Where Main Street had been, Karl could make out the dim shapes of the bank, and the Presbyterian Church. The great stone Methodist Church was still standing too.

Then suddenly the water started to move again. Next to the stone bridge, the embankment had given way. The water raged through the hole, past the bridge. The lake covering the city began to go down.

After a few minutes, Karl saw people crawling across the wreckage. Some were trying to make their way to the hills. Others were heading toward the few buildings that were left standing in what had been Johnstown less than an hour ago.

"Karl, what should we do?" His mother's low voice came from beside him out of the darkness. "We must help somehow."

Karl took her hand. "I don't know how we can help yet, mother. It's getting dark. We have no light. It will be very dangerous." He put an arm around his mother's shoulders.

They crouched beside each other in the darkness, with the rain still falling. Gertrude held Anna close, trying to

warm her. Gradually the baby quieted and slept again. It wasn't long after that that the fire began.

Down at the stone bridge, where the huge pile of debris had collected, something exploded. Perhaps a pocket of gas had caught fire. Perhaps coals from a fireplace suddenly flared. Whatever the cause, flames began to move through the huge mass of tangled wreckage. Whipped by the wind, the fire quickly spread. Hearing the screams of people who were caught in the blaze was almost too much to bear.

Karl leaned against his mother, fearful of what might happen next. He wondered what had happened to his neighbors, his school friends. Most of all, Karl wondered what had happened to his father. When the dam broke, had his father been killed? Had he been swept away by the water? Karl squeezed his eyes shut, trying to push the thought from his mind. There was nothing to do but wait for morning and the light of day.

CHAPTER 5

After the Flood

KARL'S FINGERS and toes were numb from the cold. His body ached. He hadn't slept. The cries for help coming from down below had made sleep impossible.

The fire at the stone bridge had blazed all night long. In its eerie glow, Karl had seen other people climbing up

Green Hill. He had no idea how many had passed the tree where he and his mother had taken shelter.

At long last, the rain had stopped. Off in the east, the sky was getting lighter. The sun was rising. Karl could see the outline of hills around him. As the light grew brighter, Karl looked down into Johnstown. What just yesterday had been a neat, prosperous city was now a hideous sea of mud and debris.

Karl's mother stirred beside him. Baby Anna was still asleep in her arms. Gertrude stared down at the drowned city. *"Es ist unglaublich,"* she said softly.

Yes, it was unbelievable, Karl thought. Many buildings were totally destroyed. Even the stone churches and schools had been damaged. On what had been

Washington Street, everything was gone except for the railroad station. The eastern end of Johnstown, where the Edelmann's house had stood, was nothing but a pile of wreckage. The western end of town, near the Point, was a wasteland still partly underwater. Beyond the stone bridge, the Cambria mill was in ruins. The great smokestacks had been knocked over. Several of the biggest buildings were smashed.

Here and there, Karl saw people moving around in the wreckage below. Most were heading for Green Hill. That made sense. It was the only high ground that could be reached without having to cross a river. All the bridges, except the stone bridge, had been washed away.

"Mother," Karl whispered. "Do you think Father is still alive?"

His mother bit her lip. "I don't know, Karl," she replied. "But if he is, he'll find us. In the meantime, we have to help anyone we can." His mother stood up, cradling Anna in her arms. "Look. There are people gathering farther up the hill. Perhaps they will know what to do."

But most of the people on Green Hill were in shock. Karl noticed that their eyes were glassy and their faces strangely blank. Few people spoke. Those who did talked in whispers. Almost no one was crying. The enormity of the disaster had just started to sink in.

Karl's mother had spotted a woman who had lived about a block away from them on Washington Street. Gertrude hurried over and took her hand. Karl heard his mother say something about needing water, food, and blankets. "Someone needs to care for the injured," said the other woman, "and the children."

"Karl? Karl Edelmann?" Karl turned at the sound of his name. It was Mr. Rausch. Karl barely recognized him. The young man's clothes were badly torn and covered with mud. He had terrible bruises on his face and hands. But still he smiled as he walked up to Karl and thrust out his hand. Karl took his hand and shook if firmly.

"Herr Rausch, it is so good to see you," Karl said in German. He meant every word.

Mr. Rausch smiled slightly, remembering another conversation he had had with Karl just a few days earlier. "We should go down and look for survivors, for people who are trapped in the wreckage."

Before he could even ask her, Karl's mother simply nodded. "Be very, very careful," she whispered, cupping Karl's face in her hands.

From high on Green Hill, Johnstown was just a blur of destruction. But down in the ruined city, the enormity of the disaster came into focus. Everywhere Karl looked there were crumpled buildings, upturned train cars, and broken machinery, telegraph poles, wagons, and trees.

Broken furniture, wooden planks, smashed dishes, and muddy clothing were heaped and scattered all around. He saw the bodies of horses, dogs, and cats. He saw the bodies of people, too. The sight and smell of death all around made him feel sick.

Karl and Mr. Rausch slogged through mud and crawled over wreckage. They moved slowly, looking for signs of life. They found a little girl curled up inside a barrel. How she had survived, Karl could not even imagine. Further on, they helped a man rescue an entire family that was trapped in a building that looked like it was about to collapse.

They walked past an enormous heap of bricks that had once been a house. Karl heard voices coming from the other side. There he and Mr. Rausch saw two men holding the arms of a woman. She was pinned under a huge plank. A third man had crawled beneath the board. He was using his shoulders to lift it up. Karl heard him grunt from the strain. He saw the muscles in the man's back bulge. For a moment, nothing happened. Then the plank moved. With a shout, the two other men pulled the woman free.

The man who'd raised the plank stood up slowly. Karl stopped dead in his tracks. The man was his father!

Victor Edelmann turned. He saw Karl standing there, not ten feet away. Victor ran to his son. In one swift

movement he threw his arms around Karl and lifted him into the air.

"Papa, Papa!" cried Karl, hugging his father as hard as he could.

"Karl, you're alive!" said Victor as he set his son down. Then his face grew serious. "Karl . . . your mother and Anna. Are they still alive too?"

"Yes, Papa," Karl replied hoarsely. "They're fine. They're up on Green Hill. We escaped the water, Papa. We made it just in time."

Relief washed over Victor's face. "When the dam gave way . . . Karl, I cannot tell you how frightened I was." He hugged Karl hard again.

When his father released him, Karl stared up into Victor's face. "Papa, I'm sorry. I'm sorry if you thought I was ashamed of you. You saved us, Father. We would probably all be dead if it weren't for you."

Victor put his hands on his son's shoulders. "Your mother and Anna would probably be dead if it weren't for you, Karl. I'm very proud of you."

Victor stood up. "Come, let's go find your mother. After that, we'll come back down here and see what else we can do to help."

With his arm still around Karl's shoulders, Victor turned toward Green Hill. He threw his other arm around Mr. Rausch. The younger man smiled. He and Victor began to talk in German, each man telling his own story of what happened.

Karl hung on his father's every word. It didn't matter if he spoke in German, or English, or any other language. It didn't matter if he was a steel worker or an engineer, a poor man or a rich one. Having his father safe and alive was all that mattered. Karl knew he would never forget that. He also knew that he would never forget the Johnstown flood.

The Johnstown Flood

▲ Johnstown after the flood

 THE JOHNSTOWN FLOOD of May 31, 1889, was one of the worst disasters in American history. When the South Fork Dam broke, an estimated 20 million gallons of water swept through the Little Conemaugh River valley. Fourteen miles separated the dam from Johnstown. The floodwaters hit the town at 4:07 p.m. In ten minutes, Johnstown was almost completely destroyed. Officially, 2,209 people died in the Johnstown Flood. Thousands more were injured. Many people lost their homes.

What Caused the Johnstown Flood?

Several things came together to cause the Johnstown Flood. The first was unusual weather. The rain that drenched western Pennsylvania on the night of May 30 started out as a storm in Kansas and Nebraska two days before. When it struck Pennsylvania, it was the worst storm that had ever hit that part of the state in recorded history. Heavy rain fell almost nonstop over a large area. Experts estimated that between six and eight inches of rain fell in the Johnstown area in just twenty-four hours. In that same time, as

Floodplain Diagrams

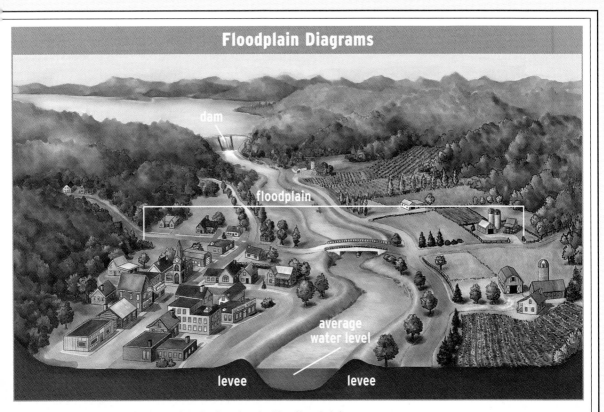

▲ The dam helps control the level of water in the floodplain.

▲ After the dam breaks, the water level in the floodplain rises. This causes the floodplain to flood.

much as ten inches fell in the mountains that surrounded the town.

The rain of May 30 added water to a landscape that was already soaked. This was a second factor that led to the flood. The spring of 1889 had been very wet in the area around Johnstown. There had already been a hundred days of rain that year. Eleven of those rainy days had been earlier in May. All that rain meant that the ground was saturated with water. The rainwater on May 30 flowed over the ground and down the hillsides instead of soaking into the soil.

The speed at which the rainwater moved toward lower ground was another problem. It might have flowed more slowly down the hillsides if the dense forests growing on the hills around Johnstown had been untouched.

But in many places, large patches of trees had been cut for lumber. The wood was burned in the huge furnaces in the town's steel mills. Where the trees had been cut, the ground was bare. There were no bushes or even grass to help slow the water. So it gushed down the hillsides, brown with dirt. The rainwater ended up in creeks and streams. These flowed into rivers such as the Little Conemaugh and Stonycreek. They overflowed their banks very quickly.

Some of those creeks flowed into Lake Conemaugh. The final and most important factor that led to the Johnstown Flood was the collapse of the South Fork Dam. Originally, the South Fork dam had been well-built. But years of neglect and bad repairs had made it unsafe. When huge amounts of water flowed into the South

▼ **Debris chokes the river beside the stone bridge in Johnstown after the flood.**

Fork Dam on May 30 and 31, 1889, the pressure was too great. The earth-and-rock face of the dam began to split in several places. Water flowing over the top of the dam cut away at the dam's face, too. Finally the dam gave way, releasing millions of gallons of water. Nothing could have stopped the fast-moving wall of water once it started to move. The water gained speed as it surged down the narrow Little Conemaugh River valley. The floodwaters also grew more destructive as they picked up and carried along everything in their path. Traveling at 40 mph, the wall of water and debris struck Johnstown 57 minutes after the South Fork Dam broke.

After the Flood

Newspaper reporters arrived at Johnstown early the next morning. Many of them had walked for miles across the hills in the rain to get there. What they found was almost beyond belief. Entire blocks of buildings had been destroyed. Enormous piles of rubble and mud stretched as far as the eye could see. And scattered throughout the ruins of Johnstown were hundreds of bodies and thousands of homeless survivors.

When news of the Johnstown Flood reached the outside world, support poured in from across the country. Donations of money arrived from every state and from fourteen other countries. Farmers and businesses brought in food, water, and medicine. People donated clothing, cookstoves, cots, and much more.

Disease was one of the greatest fears after the terrible flood. An outbreak of typhoid added 40 more deaths to those killed by the floodwaters, but the outbreak was stopped.

Clara Barton

Clara Barton, who started the American Red Cross, arrived in Johnstown with fifty doctors and nurses within a week of the flood disaster. The Johnstown Flood was the first real test of the Red Cross in the United States.

Clara Barton established her headquarters in an abandoned railroad car. She set up large tents that became hospitals. She also set up Red Cross hotels for flood survivors. Clara Barton stayed in Johnstown for five months. During that time, she worked around the clock. She and her volunteers treated the sick and injured. They distributed nearly a half million dollars' worth of blankets, food, and clothing.

The dead were buried, and the survivors slowly began putting their lives back together. The cleanup and restoration of Johnstown, however, took five years.

Many people held the members of the South Fork Hunting and Fishing Club responsible for the Johnstown Flood. But most of those members were very wealthy and powerful men. Several lawsuits were filed against the Club by people who had lost family members in the disaster. In the end, neither the Club, nor any of its members, were held responsible for the flood.

A few traces of the South Fork Dam are still visible today. The Johnston Flood Museum and the Johnstown Flood National Memorial, run by the National Park Service, tell the story of the 1889 disaster in words and pictures.

▲ People sorting through the remains of buildings after the flood

▲ The remains of Lake Conemaugh after the dam broke.

Write an Eyewitness Account

THE JOHNSTOWN FLOOD changed the lives of the people living in Johnstown. Many other floods have occurred throughout history, causing damage and destruction to the areas where they happened.

- Choose a flood that occurred in the past.

- Research the effects of the flood on the land and the people who lived near it.

- Write questions to guide your research. Then write on note cards the related information you find.

- Use the information you gather to write an eyewitness account of the flood. Write as if you were someone who witnessed the flood.

What did you do to prepare for the flood?

How did you feel during the flood?

How did people recover from the flood?

What type of damage did the flood cause?

Read More About Floods

FIND AND READ more books about floods. As you read, think about these questions. They will help you understand more about this topic.

- What are some causes of floods?

- Can you name some of the major floods in history?

- Can scientists predict when a flood will occur? What instruments do they use?

- What are some of the benefits of floods?

- Why can floods be dangerous?

SUGGESTED READING
Reading Expeditions
Earth Science:
The Wonders of Water

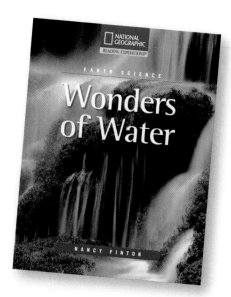